C000057413

Plas Mawr, Conwy

Rick Turner MA, FSA

'A Worthy Plentiful House'

Plas Mawr, or the 'Great Hall' as its name unashamedly announces, is one of the grandest and most ambitious houses ever raised in a Welsh historic town. Built in the heart of prosperous sixteenth-century Conwy, the earliest plasterwork at Plas Mawr bears the date 1577 — the year in which Francis Drake set out on his circumnavigation of the globe. It is a dwelling of noble proportions, where the decoration and design betray clear signs of its creator's experiences, travels, and links with the court circle. At the same time, it is a building that displays traits that are typical of the Tudor Renaissance style as it emerged in Wales. So unspoilt are its glorious features, Plas Mawr stands today as the finest surviving town house of the Elizabethan era (1558–1603) to be found anywhere in the British Isles.

This 'worthy plentiful house' was the creation of Robert Wynn (d. 1598), whose initials — R. W. — appear so frequently on its ornamental plasterwork. Born as the third son of a modestly well-to-do north Wales family, whose home lay at Gwydir in the Conwy valley, the prospects for Wynn's career would not have looked particularly auspicious. He was, however, to lead a full and remarkable life, rising as one of the brightest stars among the gentry of Tudor Wales.

Robert Wynn eventually settled in Conwy, which, even as late as the mid-sixteenth century, still remained in essence an English borough. Although Welshmen had long infiltrated these bastions of alien settlement and influence in north Wales, as late as 1506 they were still forbidden to own land within the town. But Wynn was clearly a man of talent and substance, and one who was willing to seize the opportunities presented to him. He became, too, a person of taste and experience, and he chose to invest greatly in his new house and its lavish decoration. Plas Mawr was to become a bold reflection and display of the position Robert Wynn held in late sixteenth-century Welsh society.

By the late 1630s, the house had been inherited by Wynn's grandson, who was also named Robert. Following his death in 1664, a very full inventory was taken of the house and its contents. This document has provided much of the evidence for the way in which Plas Mawr is presented to visitors today.

Opposite: Repainted in its true heraldic colours, the plaster overmantel in the hall is a vivid and bright reminder of the Elizabethan era. For Robert Wynn, it was an opportunity to proclaim his descent from princely stock and to impress his visitors with his wealth and status.

Below: Visitors to Plas Mawr passed through the gatehouse into the lower courtyard, then climbed the steps to enter the hall, as indeed they do today.

Robert Wynn

The rise in the fortunes of the Wynn family was begun by Robert's grandfather, Maredudd ab Ieuan ap Robert (d. 1525), the son of a freeholder of Eifionydd, near Caernarfon. Maredudd had the courage to take a lease on royal bond lands in the remote uplands of Dolwyddelan. Here he converted the ruinous thirteenth-century castle into a home for his new bride, Alice. Maredudd cleared the area of notorious bandits and planted his followers in new farms around the township, and from these fragile beginnings his fortunes grew. Maredudd steadily increased his land holdings into the Conwy valley and ended his days in 1525, surrounded by many of his twenty-one children in his new house at nearby Gwydir.

His eldest son, John Wyn ap Maredudd (d. 1559), inherited most of the estate and continued to prosper, particularly after the suppression of the monasteries in 1536–40. John acquired most of the lands of the former Cistercian abbey of Aberconwy (Maenan). He, in turn, had seven children, five boys and two girls. Morus (d. 1580) and Gruffudd, the two elder sons, were to establish separate lines of the family. Born at Gwydir about 1520, Robert Wynn was his third son.

As such, Robert had few prospects of inheriting his father's estate. Thus, like many of his contemporaries of similar station, he was to enter the household of a man with more power than that of his own family. First he was to serve Sir Walter Stonor (d. 1550), lieutenant of the Tower of London. Sir Walter's daughter married a rising favourite at court, Philip Hoby (1505–58), and Robert Wynn was to move with her into Hoby's household.

If we are to trace Robert's career over the succeeding years, we have to follow the better-documented life of Sir Philip Hoby. Hoby was a member of a Herefordshire gentry family. His zeal for the Protestant faith was to commend him to Henry VIII (1509–47), and he was appointed as one of the gentlemen serving in the king's privy chamber. Between 1535 and 1538, Hoby was sent on various diplomatic missions on behalf of the Crown, and in 1544 he took part in King Henry's three-month siege of Boulogne. We know that Robert Wynn took part in this siege and it was there that he received a wound in his leg, which was to trouble him for the rest of his life. As a reward for his bravery at Boulogne, Philip Hoby was knighted and given property in London.

Sir Philip became Master of the Ordnance in the north and in 1544 he was to help lead the king's Scottish campaigns. Robert was present at the winning and burning of Edinburgh and Leith.

Above: A memorial brass in Dolwyddelan Church showing Maredudd ab Ieuan ap Robert (d. 1525), Robert Wynn's grandfather.

Opposite: Restored by Maredudd in the late fifteenth century, Dolwyddelan Castle was set within royal bond lands. Maredudd's estates were the basis of the family's wealth.

Below: Gwydir Castle was begun by Maredudd and later completed by his heir, John Wyn ap Maredudd (d. 1559). Robert Wynn was born here about 1520.

Right: Sir Philip Hoby drawn by Hans Holbein the younger (1497–1543). Robert spent his early career in the service of Sir Philip (The Royal Collections © 2007, Her Majesty Queen Elizabeth II).

Below: The family of Henry VIII painted in about 1572 by Lucas de Heere (1534–84). Henry VIII (1509–47) is seated on the royal throne, his son, Edward VI (1547–53), is kneeling at his left hand, his elder daughter, Mary I (1553–58), and her husband, Philip II of Spain (d. 1598), are standing to his right and Elizabeth I (1558–1603) is to his left (National Museum of Wales).

Right: Bachegraig, the house built by Sir Richard Clough in 1567 in the Renaissance style, is thought to have been the first brick house in Wales. This watercolour by Moses Griffith is taken from Thomas Pennant's Tour in Wales (1786) (National Library of Wales).

After King Henry's death in 1547, Hoby was to serve his son, Edward VI (1547–53). Indeed, he was made ambassador to the court of Charles V, the Holy Roman Emperor, and the most important ruler in Europe. In 1551, Sir Philip Hoby was sent with the marquess of Northumberland to negotiate a marriage between Edward VI and Elizabeth, daughter of King Henry II of France. On his departure, he was attended by 'ten gentlemen of his owne, in velvet cotes and chaines of gold'. Robert Wynn was quite probably among this distinguished party.

Much of Hoby's next three years was spent as an ambassador in Flanders, at Antwerp or Brussels, and in the company of Sir Thomas Gresham (d. 1579). Gresham's secretary was Sir Richard Clough (d. 1570), a Denbighshire man, who made his fortune trading from Flanders before returning home to build the sophisticated and innovative new houses of Bachegraig and Plas Clough.

Following the death of Edward VI in 1553, Queen Mary (1553–58) recalled Sir Philip Hoby to England because of supposed links to the ill-fated Lady Jane Grey (d. 1554). Soon, however, he was to return to the Continent and again to take up the post of ambassador in Brussels. In 1554, he fell ill whilst travelling to Padua in Italy to take the waters and to meet his friends, the painter, Titian (d. 1576), and his flamboyant patron, Pietro Aretino (d. 1556). Sir Philip returned home in 1556, and he died in London two years later. He was buried in the parish church at Bisham in Berkshire, his country estate. A magnificent memorial survives in the church, and commemorates both Sir Philip and his brother, Thomas (d. 1566).

Unfortunately, the role Robert Wynn played in the household of Sir Philip Hoby is not clear. Robert will, however, have been present at some of the major battles of the Tudor period. He will have travelled to the most lavish courts in northern Europe and he would have worked in the richest commercial cities of the day. Robert was to return to his home in north Wales with the memories, influences and possibly some of

The Seven Wonders of Bruges, *attributed to P. Claessens the elder (1499–1576), about 1550. These magnificent buildings, centred on the vast Cloth Hall — the focus of the city's wealth — would have been well known to Robert Wynn on his visits to Flanders (Monasterium de Wijngaard; Photographer Hugo Maertens, Bruges).*

the wealth accumulated over his twenty years of service in the household of a great gentleman.

Robert Wynn is first recorded in the local affairs of north Wales from the 1540s. With his father, he renewed his grandfather's leases from the Crown of the *ffriddoedd* or sheepwalks of Dolwyddelan. The rents from these lands were the basis of his future wealth. The renewal, expansion and renegotiation of leases of land continued throughout his life, and there is evidence for some sharp practice leading to disputes with his father, his brother, Morus, and his nephew, John. This led to a great deal of litigation, a feature in the life of many Tudor gentlemen who strove to make a fortune. In the 1560s, Robert Wynn owned a part share in the *Katheryn*, shipping La Rochelle wine into the port of Conwy. And in 1572 he built Bryn Moel, a typical Snowdonian stone farmhouse situated on his rural lands at Dolwyddelan. Without a substantial manorial estate, however, Robert chose to establish his principal household in the borough of Conwy.

Indeed, as his nephew, Sir John Wynn (d. 1627), was later to record, the lawyers of north Wales lived in Caernarfon, the merchants in Beaumaris and the gentlemen in Conwy.

Robert married Dorothy Griffith (d. 1586), the daughter of Sir William Griffith of Penrhyn, who served as chamberlain of north Wales, and the widow of William Williams of Cochwillan, near Bangor. Her family, it might be said, had a longer and better-established pedigree than that of the Wynns, but there were already close family ties. In fact, Dorothy's brother, William, was married to Robert's sister, Margaret, whereas her eldest son, William, was united to his other sister, Anne, and her younger son, Edmund, was wedded to his niece, Mary.

At the time of his marriage, Robert was — certainly by Tudor standards — at the advanced age of 50. But it was the need to establish a proper home for his new wife which prompted him, in 1570, to pay Hugh Mershe £200 for a 'mansion house ... with appurtenances, one garden and three orchards' in Conwy.

The memorial to Sir Philip Hoby (d. 1558) and his brother, Sir Thomas (d. 1566), in Bisham Church, Berkshire (David Nash Ford).

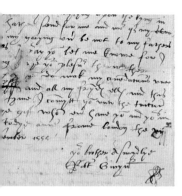

Above: In a letter to his brother Morus in 1553, Robert signed his name 'Robt Gwyn'. Following his move to Conwy, Robert was known by the more familiar name of Wynn (National Library of Wales, Ms. 9051E).

Below: The 'chamber over the parlour' has an elaborate plaster ceiling and frieze dated 1577. This was perhaps Dorothy Wynn's room.

Subsequent purchases of adjacent plots of land allowed Robert to build Plas Mawr and lay out its associated gardens between 1576 and 1585. Unfortunately, Dorothy was to enjoy the finished building for no more than a year. She died in 1586 without any children by Robert Wynn. No known portrait of Robert Wynn survives, though Thomas Pennant (d. 1798) described one that showed him 'painted in black, with a book in his hand, and with short grey hair and beard'.

It was to be quite late in his life before Robert Wynn achieved recognition. In 1570, he was commissioned to provide an armoured horseman for the queen's service. He was a justice of the peace on lists prepared in 1575 and 1581, in 1589 he sat in parliament for Caernarvonshire, and was sheriff of the county for 1590–91. Some idea of his increasing status can be seen in the way he presented his name. Early letters are signed Robert Gwyn, and legal transactions adopt the Welsh form Robert ap John ap Maredudd. Following his move to Conwy he is referred to as Robert Wynn, esquire or armiger, demonstrating that he had the right to a coat of arms.

Like many of his gentry counterparts he wanted to establish a charitable foundation. A draft will of 1588 was largely concerned with establishing a Free School in Conwy. Robert was particularly concerned that the schoolmaster be learned in 'the Arte of musycke' so that he could train eight scholars to form the choir of the parish church. He also intended to provide scholarships for four poor boys from his estates.

It was in 1588, too, that Wynn married for the second time. His new wife, Dorothy Dymock, was much younger than him. Although now in his seventies, Robert was to father two sons and five daughters within six years. This bout of remarkable fecundity so late in life had one unusual side effect, as later related by Sir John Wynn in his family's memoirs.

'Some six years after his last marriage his body, being stirred in getting children at those years (untimely for that purpose), his wanted

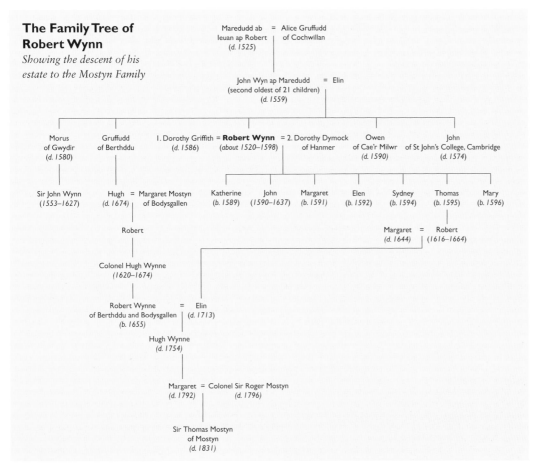

The Family Tree of Robert Wynn

Showing the descent of his estate to the Mostyn Family

Maredudd ab Ieuan ap Robert (d. 1525) = Alice Gruffudd of Cochwillan

John Wyn ap Maredudd (second oldest of 21 children) (d. 1559) = Elin

- Morus of Gwydir (d. 1580)
- Gruffudd of Berthddu
- 1. Dorothy Griffith (d. 1586) = **Robert Wynn** (about 1520–1598) = 2. Dorothy Dymock of Hanmer
- Owen of Cae'r Milwr (d. 1590)
- John of St John's College, Cambridge (d. 1574)

Sir John Wynn (1553–1627)

Hugh (d. 1674) = Margaret Mostyn of Bodysgallen

Katherine (b. 1589) · John (1590–1637) · Margaret (b. 1591) · Elen (b. 1592) · Sydney (b. 1594) · Thomas (b. 1595) · Mary (b. 1596)

Robert

Margaret (d. 1644) = Robert (1616–1664)

Colonel Hugh Wynne (1620–1674)

Robert Wynne of Berthddu and Bodysgallen (b. 1655) = Elin (d. 1713)

Hugh Wynne (d. 1754)

Margaret (d. 1792) = Colonel Sir Roger Mostyn (d. 1796)

Sir Thomas Mostyn of Mostyn (d. 1831)

The arms of Robert Wynn (top) in the parlour, and the quartered arms of the Wynn and Griffith families (above) in the chamber over the brewhouse.

inflation took him in the leg extraordinary vehemence so that he supposed it would endanger his life.'

A surgeon was called who, on probing the wound, removed the lead from the bullet Robert had received at the siege of Boulogne some fifty years before, and which had left him lame ever since.

Robert Wynn died in 1598 and was buried in a rather plain tomb chest in the chancel of St Mary's Church in Conwy. He had had to rewrite his will to provide for his wife and his infant children from the future rents from his leased lands. All thought of a memorial Free School had to be abandoned. The management of his estates and the terms of his will led to a legal dispute that ran until 1630. This was to prove a significant factor in keeping Plas Mawr almost unaltered to the present day.

Part of the memorial slab (below) to Dorothy Wynn (née Griffith) and Robert Wynn's tomb chest (left). Both are in the chancel of St Mary's Church (By kind permission of the Vicar, St Mary's Church, Conwy).

The Building of Plas Mawr

The borough of Conwy was established by King Edward I (1272–1307), with its earliest charter granted in 1284. Enclosed by its fine town walls, and protected by the massive royal castle, the borough provided a secure base for prosperous trade by English merchants and craftsmen. The town was divided into rectangular blocks by a grid of four major and several minor streets. The blocks were then further subdivided into individual burgage or house plots rented to the new immigrant settlers. Aberconwy House, the last surviving late medieval dwelling in the town, gives an impression of the size of these early houses.

Phases of Construction

When Robert Wynn bought the 'mansion house' from Hugh Mershe in 1570, he acquired an already substantial property. It occupied the middle burgage plot fronting what was then Jugler's Lane, now Crown Lane. In 1576, Robert acquired the plot to the north, situated on the corner of Pepper Street, now Chapel Street. This enabled him to begin to build Plas Mawr. The north range of the house, dated 1576 on the outside, and whose plasterwork was completed in 1577, was an addition to the existing mansion. It contained two main bedrooms, a kitchen–brewhouse, a parlour, and accommodation for servants. When, in 1580, Robert came to complete the main house by adding the central and southern ranges, the earlier block would have provided a self-contained apartment during the building work. Mershe's house was demolished, and the full extent of the new house achieved. Access was gained via a porch on Jugler's Lane and from here a passage led into the upper courtyard. The full magnificence of the main elevation would have been hidden in such a narrow street.

It was not until 1585 that Wynn acquired the corner plot, which lay on High Street to the south. The property here had been owned by Robert Laythwood, who had no doubt stood out for an inflated price. This acquisition allowed Robert Wynn to build his gatehouse as a bold architectural statement facing directly onto Conwy's main thoroughfare. Wynn's visitors would now have entered Plas Mawr via the gatehouse, up the steps in the lower courtyard, and through a newly created doorway into the hall. Further minor acquisitions of land allowed Robert to build the dairy on the west side of the upper courtyard, and to create formal gardens to the north of the main dwelling. Robert also owned a barn, orchards and gardens outside the town walls, and he had rights to graze his animals on the town fields.

The piecemeal acquisition of various parcels of land led to a staged programme of construction. We should remember, however, that the

The main elevation of Plas Mawr, in Crown Lane. Until the gatehouse was built, visitors would have entered through the ornate door now hidden inside the porch.

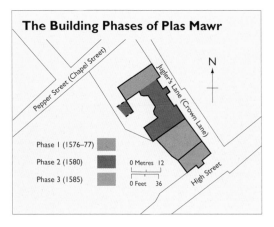

The Building Phases of Plas Mawr

Pepper Street (Chapel Street)

Jugler's Lane (Crown Lane)

N

High Street

Phase 1 (1576–77)
Phase 2 (1580)
Phase 3 (1585)

0 Metres 12
0 Feet 36

Opposite: This magnificent 'bird's-eye view' of Conwy was drawn by an unknown artist about 1600. At the time, the borough was still dominated by the castle and town walls, but Plas Mawr, with its gatehouse and formal garden, is clearly shown as the most prominent house in the town (By permission of the marquess of Salisbury, Hatfield House, CPM 1/62).

Right: This elevation of a house, and part of its plan, was the work of John Thorpe (about 1563–1655). Drawn about 1612, it is thought to be a preliminary design for Campden House, Kensington (Sir John Soane's Museum, London).

Below: The frontispiece of one of the most influential early books on architecture, Tutte l'Opere d'Architettura, published in Venice by Sebastiano Serlio (1475–1554) and widely available in England from the mid-sixteenth century (British Library).

profession of architect was not properly established in Elizabethan times. Robert may therefore have commissioned a 'plot' or ground plan, and perhaps a main elevation from a mason in the royal works or perhaps in favour at court. He may also have acquired a number of Flemish or Italian architectural books from which decorative details could be drawn. Wynn might also be expected to have drawn upon his own experience of the architecture of much of northern Europe as well as the design of Bisham Abbey, Philip Hoby's house (his patron). Armed with this information, he would have instructed a local master mason or master carpenter to supervise the different stages of the building programme. This approach probably explains the unity of the plan of the main house, but the difference in the details of the north range from the remainder.

Plas Mawr lies on a sloping site, which had to be cut into three terraces to take the different phases of building. The burgage plots themselves may already have been continuously occupied for some three centuries and any earlier buildings would now have been swept away. A systematic network of drains was laid out to cope with the problem of groundwater.

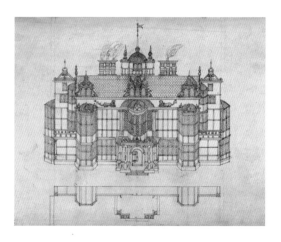

Building Skills

Four main building trades were involved in the overall construction: masons, carpenters, plasterers and slaters; with specialist carvers, glaziers and painters also required to add the finishing details.

Masons

The rubble stone for the walls came from the hills behind the town and the finer stone for the dressings around the doors and windows was brought from Deganwy on

Phase I: 1578–79

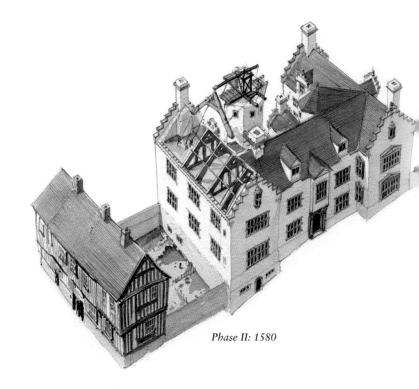

Phase II: 1580

the opposite side of the Conwy estuary. When we compare the details of the north range with those of the remainder of the house, it is clear that there are variations in the design of the windows and other features. This implies that a different mason was responsible for the two phases.

Carpenters

Plas Mawr retains a wealth of heavy carpentry in its floor structures, its screens and its massive roof trusses. Most of this woodwork carries a series of carpenters' marks, showing that the various features were prefabricated in a 'framing yard', away from the house, and then brought on site for assembly. For the carpenters working in the confined spaces in the middle of Conwy, this must have made raising these heavy wooden structures by block and tackle on timber scaffolding a difficult task. Several varying styles of carpenters' marks occur, so that it is possible to trace the work of different craftsmen around the house.

Some features — including the so-called double pegging of the roof trusses — are unknown beyond Plas Mawr and several contemporary buildings in the Conwy valley, which may imply that one master craftsman was used to oversee the entire project. Moreover, the style of the decorated screens in the north range of the house bears a close resemblance to work in similar structures surviving in fifteen other houses and two churches in north Wales. All of these other examples can be dated between 1571 and 1590. The name of the Welsh master craftsman responsible is unknown, but Plas Mawr is undoubtedly a powerful testament to his skill. Tree-ring dating has revealed that most of the timber used in the house was felled no more than a year or two before it was required. All of it seems to have been derived from trees growing higher up the Conwy valley.

Plasterers

The plastering of houses, and particularly the use of decorative plasterwork, was introduced to England by King Henry VIII. Highly fashionable, and at first restricted by taste and finances to the noble or courtier classes, its use slowly moved down the social scale during the second half of the sixteenth century. By the 1570s it

Carpenters' marks on the joists, made in the 'framing yard', helped them to assemble the timbers correctly on site.

Below left: Three drawings which attempt to reconstruct the principal stages in the building of Plas Mawr.

Phase I: 1578–79
The north range was begun in 1576 and decorated in 1577. This drawing also shows that the central and south ranges had been set out following the demolition of Hugh Mershe's house. To the left (south) a house owned by Robert Laythwood (probably medieval and timber framed) stood on the eventual site of the Plas Mawr gatehouse.

Phase II: 1580
The central and south ranges were completed about this date. Robert Wynn had not yet been able to purchase Robert Laythwood's house.

Phase III: 1585
By this date Robert Laythwood's house had been acquired and the gatehouse built. The house is shown largely as it survives today.

(Illustrations by Terry Ball, 1997).

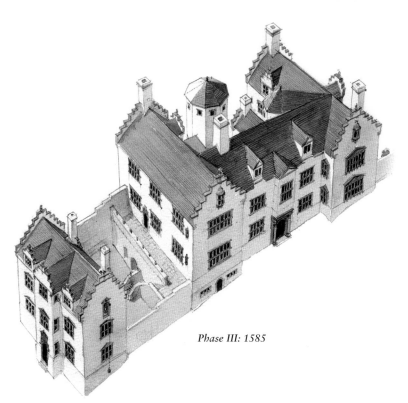

Phase III: 1585

At Maenan Hall, in the Conwy valley, the plasterers who had worked at Plas Mawr redecorated the ancient cruck-framed hall in 1582.

A detail of the gatehouse roof showing the grey Ffestiniog slates in various sizes, laid in diminishing courses alongside a slated valley.

was beginning to be adopted by the gentry and the merchant classes. Plasterwork provided a relatively cheap method of finishing the growing number of rooms in these middle-class houses. The moulded and cast decoration could be painted to imitate carved wood, or even the exotic stone decoration used in the more magnificent courtier houses. It was a way of introducing lots of colour and emblematic devices, both so beloved by the Elizabethans, into the internal decoration of their homes. Plas Mawr has long been recognized as an early and almost complete survival of this type of decoration.

Plasterers were itinerant craftsmen, often moving as a group: one master, two journeymen and several apprentices. Robert Wynn may have had to go as far as London to obtain their services. By identifying the individual emblems used in different schemes, it is possible to trace the movements of the group that came to work at Plas Mawr. They arrived at the house in 1577, probably went to work on undated schemes recorded at Robert's family house of Gwydir, and returned to Plas Mawr in 1580. In 1582 they redecorated the hall at Maenan Hall, the home of Wynn's cousin, Maurice Kyffin (d. 1598). Interestingly, many of the same motifs used by this group of plasterers

were to reappear at a house in St Peter's Street at Ipswich in Suffolk, dating to about 1600. Nearly all the walls of Plas Mawr were plastered internally and rendered externally, perhaps accounting for up to 100 tons of lime plaster in total, and with many bundles of animal hair mixed into it to bind it together.

Slaters

Slating was the fourth of the main craft skills employed during the construction of Plas Mawr. We should bear in mind, however, that over the past four hundred years, the house may have had four or perhaps even more replacement roof coverings; the original slating is lost to us. Nevertheless, from nooks and crannies within the house, some of the original head-pegged grey slates, a few oak pegs and split oak laths have been recovered, and these have revealed details of how the first roof was constructed. A French nobleman named Creton remarked on a visit to the town by King Richard II in 1399 'that at Conway … there is much slate on the houses'. In 1570, Sion Tudur complained that a thatched roof was cold for a man of station and that red slates were the fittest roof for such a man's house. So for a man of Robert Wynn's aspirations, slate was the only choice and his extensive estates in Dolwyddelan were a source of the grey Ffestiniog type of slate employed in the building.

The slaters would have been responsible for quarrying, carting and then shipping the slate down the river Conwy, as well as laying the roof. For the Elizabethan roof, many different sizes of slate would have been selected, just as in the new roof on the house, where a total of forty-three different sizes has been used. When Plas Mawr required reroofing during the eighteenth century, the slaters left a tally etched into the plaster of the south range attic: a total of 66,203 slates was used. Head-pegged Welsh slate roofs are now a great rarity and there is a danger that the evidence of this craft, which pre-dated what became a world-famous industry, will be lost for ever.

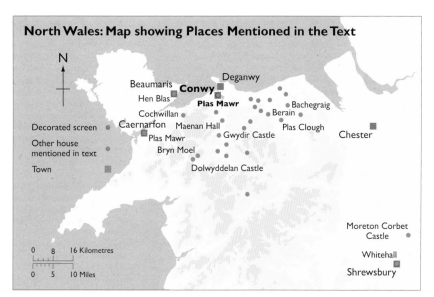

North Wales: Map showing Places Mentioned in the Text

N

Beaumaris   **Conwy**   Deganwy

Hen Blas   **Plas Mawr**

Cochwillan   Bachegraig

Caernarfon   Berain

Decorated screen   Maenan Hall   Plas Clough

Other house   Plas Mawr   Gwydir Castle   **Chester**
mentioned in text

Bryn Moel

Town   Dolwyddelan Castle

Moreton Corbet
Castle

0   8   16 Kilometres

Whitehall

0   5   10 Miles   Shrewsbury

Building Peculiarities

It was probably the lack of any form of full-time professional supervision over the building work that led to one or two mistakes creeping into the construction. Such mistakes or oversights could be as simple as one of the carpenters not completing his task on the carving of the screen in the chamber over the parlour. The most puzzling part of the building, however, may now seem a peculiarity since it is likely to represent a planning error of somewhat greater significance. It is a riddle that concerns the roof of the house.

The plaster ceiling of the great chamber is the largest and most elaborate at Plas Mawr, and it bears the date 1580. Directly above this ceiling is an elegant timber roof, with great arch-braced collar trusses, chamfered and pierced, and clearly intended to be seen and admired. It is a style of roof that was commonly found in north Wales churches and great houses from the mid-fifteenth century until the early sixteenth century. Thus, it is something of a surprise to learn that tree-ring dating has shown that the timber for the Plas Mawr roof was felled as late as 1578, just before it was needed for the construction of the house. As they rest on the east wall of the building, the ends of the huge trusses rest on pairs of timbers running right along the wall-top. But on the opposite wall, the feet of two of the trusses are buried in the stonework of the stair towers, and these form very ugly connections.

Considered as a whole, the evidence would appear to suggest that Robert Wynn originally intended to have his great chamber open to the decorated wooden roof. The carpenter was instructed and then began to make up the roof somewhere away from the site. He chose to use a regional style with which he was familiar or copied the roof surviving at Robert's father's house at Gwydir. Meanwhile, the mason built up the walls of the house, adding and raising the stair towers. Since he

is unlikely to have had accurate drawings, he perhaps did not realize the towers would rise up through part of the roof space. Inevitably, the roof would no longer look elegant. One might imagine a heated debate, but a solution had to be found. In the end, the plasterer was called in to install a ceiling that would hide the unfortunate compromise above.

Above: The decorated arch-braced collar trusses above the great chamber. Notice that the furthest truss is awkwardly cut away by the stair tower, to the right of the picture. Note also the use of two rows of pegs at the joints. This system of 'double pegging' is a distinctive feature of the house and is unknown beyond Plas Mawr and several contemporary buildings in the Conwy valley.

Left: The roof of the upper hall at Gwydir Castle — where Robert Wynn was born — probably provided the model for what was originally intended at Plas Mawr.

The Later History of Plas Mawr

The Seventeenth Century: The House Contents Described

On Robert Wynn's death, his wife, Dorothy, and her family continued to live in Plas Mawr. But a long legal wrangle concerning his will was to follow. His executor, Sir Roger Mostyn (d. 1642), was charged with managing Robert's rural estates. From these, he was to provide an allowance for Dorothy and a yearly sum of £20 to ensure the education and bringing up of Wynn's eldest son, John. Over a number of years, a sum of £400 was to be assembled towards the marriage money or dowry of three of his daughters, Katherine, Elen and Sydney, with the same figure for his younger son, Thomas. A further £500 was to be found for his youngest daughter, Mary.

The annual income from the estates amounted to some £220 6s. 8d. In ten years, a total of more than £2,200 had accumulated, just about covering all of the bequests in Robert's will. However, Dorothy, her new husband, William Williams of Vaynol (d. 1630), and her children charged Sir Roger Mostyn with mishandling the estates and their rental income. The dispute was to rumble on until 1630. As a consequence, for thirty years, there can have been little money to initiate any changes or improvements to Plas Mawr and its contents.

By 1637, Plas Mawr had been inherited by Robert Wynn's grandson, who was also named Robert (1616–64). He achieved some local prominence by becoming deputy mayor of Conwy, but never moved on the national or international stage like his grandfather. Following his death in 1664, an inventory of the contents of Plas Mawr was made. This has proved a most important document in naming and understanding the use of the different rooms in the house. The appraisers, who prepared the inventory, made their way in a logical route around the building and it is therefore possible to reconstruct the course that they followed. Unfortunately, the inventory does not list everything, only the small items of furniture, furnishings and other goods. Robert's will, which is associated with the inventory, explains why, since he left all his goods and belongings to his wife and elder son:

'... except all such standing Bedsteads, Tables, fformes, Dressers, cuboards, Binns and grates. My will being that they shall remayn there as heyre looms ...'.

Above: Sir Roger Mostyn (d. 1642), executor of Robert Wynn's will, shown as an elderly man in this portrait by Moses Griffith, after an original painting of 1634 (National Library of Wales).

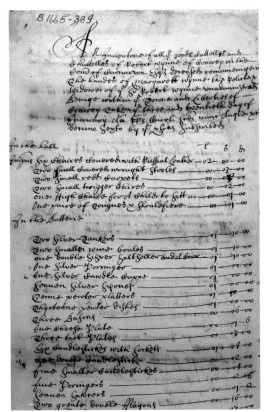

Left: An inventory of the contents of Plas Mawr was made in 1665. This section describes the contents of the hall and kitchen (National Library of Wales, Ms. B 1665/38).

Opposite: Robert Wynn's hall was no longer the great communal room of the Middle Ages. It was a room to greet visitors and occasionally hold feasts as well as a servants' dining and sitting room. The benching and large table are original to the house.

It is this inventory that has informed the decisions taken on refurnishing the hall, great chamber, kitchen, pantry, chamber over the parlour and the upper studio in the house.

In 1683, the younger Robert Wynn's daughter, Elin (d. 1713), married Robert Wynne of Bodysgallen and Berthddu. Plas Mawr was to become only the third most important house within her husband's extensive estate. From that time, it is not likely to have been lived in much by the family. In turn, the Wynnes were to marry into the Mostyn family and it is the present Lord Mostyn who remains the freeholder of Plas Mawr.

The Eighteenth and Nineteenth Centuries

During the eighteenth and nineteenth centuries, Plas Mawr was subdivided and rented out for a variety of uses. In the eighteenth century, part of the gatehouse was used as a courthouse and the house itself was let to poor families. A correspondent to the *Gentleman's Magazine* records that in 1770 an upper room contained a collection of female clothing, cases of high hats and several bows, as well as an old bedstead. By this time, much of the original contents had been stolen or removed.

The census returns, trade directories and rentals of the nineteenth century give a much more detailed picture of who was living and working in Plas Mawr. From 1839 until 1886, the white and great chambers were occupied as a school for infants, with two of the teachers and a caretaker renting rooms in the gatehouse. The school caused some problems for the other main tenant, Joseph Williams, along with his family and servants. Williams began his career as a joiner but later became a farmer and dairyman. His wife, Elizabeth, complained that the children threw stones into the milk churns in the yard, and one of their servants fell through the ceiling of the great chamber into the schoolroom. Elsewhere in the main house lived Jane Roberts, a washerwoman, and her two sons; a labourer; a railwayman; and two families called Jones. Indeed, in the 1881 census, twenty-five people were recorded as living at Plas Mawr and the house also accommodated the school and two businesses. One of the businesses was run by Thomas Thomas, a saddler, and in part of the gatehouse the Owens and later the Williams family were joiners and cabinet makers.

Surprisingly, two hundred years of multiple occupation has left relatively little impact upon Plas Mawr. Some rooms were partitioned

A view of the upper courtyard in 1802, drawn by W. Alexander (1767–1816). At the time, Plas Mawr had been divided into tenements (National Museum of Wales).

into smaller spaces and a staircase was created. The new porch and alcove above it were added on Crown Lane, and windows were bricked up. There are, however, one or two more subtle traces of these tenancies. The surviving attic doors, for example, have numbers painted on them, and in the kitchen and the red chamber there are traces of wall painting designed to imitate wallpapers of the late eighteenth century. Several ceilings were replaced and some new ceilings added to the formerly exposed beams and joists. Trapped between these new ceilings and the floors above were many hundreds of objects, either dumped in the voids or having slipped between the floorboards, and these give an indication of how the rooms were used at the time. In the great chamber, for instance, conservation works led to the discovery of hundreds of slate pencils, a few ruled school slates, and marbles and other toys dropped by the children.

Restoration and Conservation

In the later nineteenth century, senior figures within the Royal Cambrian Academy of Art, led by Clarence Whaite, grew concerned about the condition and future of Plas Mawr. In 1885, they proposed that the Academy take on the building as its headquarters. Up to that time, the Academy had held its exhibitions in different parts of Wales and a need was felt for a permanent home. Negotiations continued for two years, and in 1887 Lord Mostyn offered the Academy a thirty-year renewable lease, on condition that its members 'keep the building in the same state of repair'. The Academy appointed Arthur Baker (1842–97) and his young nephew, Herbert Baker (1862–1946) — later an assistant to Edwin Lutyens (1869–1944) and an eminent architect in his own right — as their honorary architects. During 1885, the Bakers prepared a very detailed survey of the house and its decoration,

Above: A view into the refurnished attic room, as occupied by Jane Roberts and her two sons in about 1870.

Left: A Victorian photograph of the infant pupils and one of their teachers, taken in the upper courtyard. The school occupied several rooms at Plas Mawr between 1839 and 1886 (Hugh Pritchard).

NORTH BLOCK

SOUTH BLOCK

EAST ELEVATION.

Above: The main Crown Lane elevation of Plas Mawr, drawn by Arthur and Herbert Baker in 1885.

The gatehouse seen at the end of the last century, soon after the Royal Cambrian Academy of Art took over the building (Crown Copyright: Royal Commission on the Ancient and Historical Monuments of Wales).

which was published three years later. Their volume has provided an extremely valuable record in subsequent campaigns of repairs and conservation. Interestingly, Herbert Baker was to write in his autobiography that his youthful experience at Plas Mawr was to foster a 'tendency to employ heraldry and symbols' in the decoration of his buildings.

In 1896, the Academy built the Victoria Gallery, a large brick and wooden building originally attached to the north-west corner of the house but demolished in 1995. The gallery was opened with a grand fancy dress ball held throughout Plas Mawr. Regular exhibitions of members' work were hung in all of the main rooms of the house and the gallery, and the house was open to visitors. A collection of local furniture was assembled and displayed. A series of curator–secretaries was appointed, the first at Plas Mawr being a local man, the impressive Mr J. R. Furness

(d. 1921) who worked for the Academy for thirty-three years. It was Mr Furness who supervised the erection of the diamond jubilee weathervane, wrote the early guidebooks to the house and began the conservation of the plasterwork. The celebrated journal, *Country Life*, featured the house in its pages in 1908, and the importance of Plas Mawr as a remarkable Elizabethan dwelling became properly recognized.

Arthur and Herbert Baker must have undertaken some of the works to remove evidence for the subdivision of the house into tenements and they made general repairs to the fabric. For the Academy, a voluntary body, it became a constant battle to keep the building maintained. From the late 1940s, the minute books of the Academy record ever-increasing expenditure on the buildings. The dressed stonework of the windows and doorways was very badly decayed, and leaks were a serious problem. Weaknesses in the timber beams in the cellars and the roofs required propping and tying together, and the decorated ceilings became detached from the joists that supported them.

All in all, although Plas Mawr had remained almost unaltered since its construction by Robert Wynn in the late sixteenth century, it had also gone largely without maintenance of any great scale. With grant-aid from the Ministry of Works and charitable trusts, and with money raised from its own resources, the Royal Cambrian Academy of Art spent nearly forty years making what repairs it could. Eventually, the scale of work became too great. In 1993 the Academy moved next door into its new headquarters in the converted Seion Chapel and Lord Mostyn placed Plas Mawr in guardianship of the State. Cadw, the historic environment service of the Welsh Assembly Government, subsequently undertook the complete conservation of the house and now maintains Plas Mawr as one of the finest Elizabethan townhouses in Britain.

Left: The great chamber hung with an exhibition of paintings (Copyright: National Monuments Record of Wales — Una Norman Collection).

Below: A view of the south range roof being dismantled, prior to renovation — one aspect of Cadw's extensive conservation work at Plas Mawr (Photograph by K. Hoverd).

The Working of the Household

The Tudor Household

Likewise in the houses of Knights, gentlemen, merchantmen, and some other wealthy citizens, it is not geason (uncommon) to behold generally their great provision of tapestry. Turkey work, pewter, brass, fine linen, and thereto costly cupboards of plate.

The Description of England, William Harrison (1577).

William Harrison's observations on Elizabethan households remind us that the bare rooms created by Robert Wynn at Plas Mawr served as mere shells — spaces in which he might display his wealth, his pedigree and connections, and in which he could play host to his family and friends. Indeed, the value of the contents in the rooms at Wynn's Plas Mawr was probably equivalent to the sum he invested in the construction of the house. It is both the building and its contents that provide the context for understanding the working of a great late sixteenth-century household.

A Tudor household was a carefully structured organization, treated by its master almost as an extended family. The largest and most complex household of all was the royal court. Here the principal servants were lords of the realm, each controlling a huge budget and an enormous staff. Access to the monarch and senior courtiers was strictly controlled and the royal palaces were carefully planned to enable different levels of the household to act independently. Service in the royal household was an honour. It provided a position of influence — the key to wealth — with offices often passing from father to son.

The great magnates of the realm also maintained huge households, with personnel numbering up to two hundred or more. In some cases, the size of the household competed with the court itself. Robert Wynn began his career as part of the household of Sir Walter Stonor and for much of his adult life he served in that of Sir Philip Hoby, where he would have observed the great courts of Europe at work. Within his own household at Plas Mawr, Robert would no doubt have adapted these practices to his own circumstances.

Opposite: The kitchen refurnished with its formidable batterie de cuisine, a mixture of original and replica items, described in the 1665 inventory of the contents of Plas Mawr.

Below: Queen Elizabeth I in procession, about 1600. This painting typifies the structure and hierarchy of the royal court. The group is led by Knights of the Garter and supervised by the Earl of Worcester, Master of the Horse. Grooms of the Litter push the queen, followed by ladies-in-waiting and guarded by Gentlemen Pensioners (Private Collection).

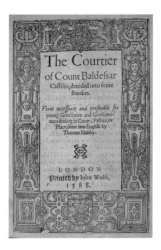

The title page of the 1588 edition of The Book of the Courtier, *by Baldesar Castiglione (d. 1529). It was translated and first published in English by Sir Thomas Hoby in 1561.*

Sets of household regulations survive from Tudor times, setting out the duties of each servant and how they were to behave towards their master, his family and guests. Such regulations were supplemented by printed books of 'nurture', 'dietary' and 'courtesy', which provided practical guides on how a gentleman should behave and look after himself and his household. Most of these books of manners derive from works published in the Renaissance courts of Italy, the most influential being *The Book of the Courtier* by Baldesar Castiglione (d. 1529), translated and first published in English in 1561 by Sir Philip Hoby's brother, Sir Thomas.

The definition of a gentleman, like Robert Wynn, was someone of wealth and leisure. Every gentleman therefore needed servants to run his household and his estate. The two surviving versions of Robert Wynn's will provide an indication of the make-up of his household. Robert showed particular favour to his nephew, Richard Wynn (d. 1617), later archdeacon of Bangor. This implies that Richard was the principal servant, best regarded as a steward or secretary. Robert made grants of land to Rhydderch ap Robert and his son, Humphrey ap Rhydderch, both of whom he referred to as 'my man'. On the occasion of her marriage, marking the end of her service, Robert gave a substantial dowry of cattle to Dorothy Hookes, who had perhaps acted as a lady-in-waiting to Dorothy, his wife. He gave the same to Margaret ferch Ithel at her marriage and she was referred to as 'my maid'. Finally, to his men servants in livery, who dwelt in Plas Mawr, he gave two cattle, or double their annual wages. And to every woman servant dwelling in the house, one cow or double her annual wage. Livery refers not only to the colourful uniform the male servants would have worn, but also to the daily ration of food and drink to which the whole household was entitled, in addition to their modest wages. Taken together, this implies that the household at Plas Mawr comprised between eleven and twenty servants.

Right: The pantry in which dry goods, meat and game were stored before being transferred to the kitchen.

The Servant Rooms and their Functions

Considering the planning and arrangements at Plas Mawr, we can see where the servants lived and worked. The gatehouse had a suite of rooms at ground- and first-floor levels, which was set aside for the steward, Richard Wynn. He would have administered Robert Wynn's household, rural estates and financial transactions. The isolated room alongside the gatehouse passage (now the ticket point and shop) was for the porter, who controlled the main entrance, and greeted and announced visitors.

In the main house, the two cellars were where the wine and beer were stored. The rear cellar contains a large boiler either for providing hot water for laundry, or for cooking the daily pottage (a thick soup) or boiled meats, the staple diet of the household. The cellar was reached from the buttery, the province of the butler, and it was in the buttery that drink was put into flagons and pitchers to be taken

to the table. All the valuable silver and pewter plate, and the candlesticks, were also stored in this room to be distributed around the house as required.

By the end of the Elizabethan period, and certainly by 1665 (the date chosen for the current displays in the furnished rooms), the hall was no longer the main family room at Plas Mawr. It would have been used as the servants' dining and sitting room, overseen by 'my man', Rhydderch ap Robert. Most of the remainder of the ground floor was occupied by rooms concerned with the production of food and drink. The kitchen had a huge *batterie de cuisine* for the cook, perhaps two or three undercooks, and a boy to turn the spits in the rack. All the dry goods, flour, grain, bread, salt, bacon and so on, together with the meat and game, were stored and partly prepared in the pantry. Water came from the well in the courtyard. The cook may also have been responsible for brewing and baking in the brewhouse. The dairy was where the butter and cheese were made, and from the equipment listed in the 1665 inventory, we

know it acted as the laundry. Robert Wynn had cows grazing on the town fields, so fresh milk would come in twice a day. He also owned orchards and gardens both inside and outside the walls, and a barn, where sacks of grain, fodder and perhaps his horses were kept. His family leased a fishtrap in the estuary.

Taken together, these facilities would have provided a wide range of fresh foods and their preparation would have been the responsibility of many more servants. Conwy was a small town, and although it had a weekly market it could not provide many of the staple foods required by such a large household. Wynn's steward would certainly have ordered more unusual and exotic foods — items such as spices, sultanas and sugar — from merchants trading as far afield as Chester and Beaumaris.

In its planning, Plas Mawr provided for far greater efficiency in the storage, preparation and distribution of food and drink than had been the case in medieval castles and manor houses. William Harrison wrote in 1577 that 'the mansion houses of our country towns ...

A reconstruction of the brewhouse in the north range of Plas Mawr (Illustration by Terry Ball, 1997).

Brewing was a labour-intensive process as shown in this mid-sixteenth-century German illustration of a brewhouse. Similar activity would no doubt have been seen during brewing at Plas Mawr (British Library).

The studio in the north range lay between Robert and Dorothy Wynn's bedrooms. A servant would have slept here to be on call during the night.

have neither dairy, stable and brewhouse annexed unto them under the same roof — as in many places beyond the sea ...'. Indeed, Plas Mawr presages the growing sophistication of household planning as it developed over the next generation. In due course, service rooms were to be grouped together in sub-basements, and with separate back staircases to the family rooms above.

The attics in the north and south ranges of the building provided four substantial bedchambers for the servants. Each was set out in dormitory fashion, with the men and women sleeping in separate quarters.

The Wynn Cupboard

Above: The Wynn family arms, shown in this detail from the overmantel in the hall, appear reversed on the cupboard.

The Wynn cupboard (By kind permission of the Burrell Collection, Glasgow).

This is the most remarkable piece of furniture surviving from Tudor Wales. It was made locally for John Wyn ap Maredudd, Robert's father, around 1545, and stood in the Wynn's family home, Gwydir Castle, until 1921. The front of the cupboard, more properly termed a buffet, is wonderfully carved with heraldic devices and emblems relating to the Wynns. Many of the same emblems reappear in the plasterwork at Plas Mawr. A white linen cupboard cloth would have been laid across the shelf and all the Wynn's best silver and gilt plate placed on top as the prelude to any feast or great occasion. The top table would have been served with wine and some of the more sumptuous dishes direct from the buffet. Once the meal was finished, the plate and best linen would have been stored in the cupboards and drawers for safe keeping.

In 1921, it was sold to the American newspaper magnate and eccentric collector, William Randolph Hearst (d. 1951). It was later sold to the Scottish shipowner and collector, Sir William Burrell (d. 1958). The Wynn cupboard is now in the Burrell Collection, Glasgow, and an accurate replica is on display at Plas Mawr.

The Family Rooms

Robert and Dorothy Wynn, and their family and guests, would have occupied the rooms on the first floor of the house. Guests arriving at Plas Mawr would have entered by way of the gatehouse. From there, the route through which they would have been led demonstrated both the sophistication and the growing magnificence of the house. In the gatehouse, the Tudor Renaissance detailing is at its most successful. The royal arms are placed immediately over the outer doorway and over the inner door there is the family motto in Latin and

Greek, which translates as *Bear: Forbear*. Greeted by the porter, the guest party would be led through the courtyard and up the steps and terrace, into the hall. Today this room has been quite sparsely furnished and there is little by way of colour apart from the exuberant plaster overmantel, which proclaims the Wynn family's importance.

Either met by Robert Wynn, his steward or his man, the guests would then be led upstairs to the great chamber, the ceremonial pivot of Plas Mawr. It is the largest, best-lit and most richly furnished room in the house. Referred to as the dining room in the 1665 inventory, the fixed benching around the walls, together with

A detail from Sir Henry Unton's memorial picture, painted around 1596. Here, we see private life in an Elizabethan household. The picture shows a feast and a masque in Sir Henry's great chamber, a business meeting in his parlour, and music being played to friends in the private chamber (National Portrait Gallery).

*Robert Wynn's motto is carved
in Greek* ANEXΩ:AΠEXΩ *and
Latin* SVSTINE:ABSTINE *in
the pediment of the inner porch
doorway of the gatehouse. It is
translated* Bear:Forbear.

nineteen chairs and a leather couch, made for extensive seating arrangements.

Robert Wynn was known for keeping a 'worthy plentiful house', and as Andrew Boorde wrote in 1542 'men wyll call hym lyght-witted, to set up a great house, and is not able to kepe man nor mouse'. Giving hospitality and feasting within the great chamber would have reinforced Robert Wynn's status within his own family, as well as among the gentry and professional classes of north Wales. The preparation of the table and serving of the meals were formal occasions in which the servants in livery had specific roles. The butler would bring the carefully folded white linen cloths from the buttery to cover the tables and the cupboard. Next he would bring the principal salt cellar (Robert had a double silver one), and the carving knives to set before his master, along with a basket of bread — the upper crust — cut from the top of loaves cooked in the oven. The pewter and silver plate would be placed upon the cupboard, and a basin and towel offered to the master and then his guests to wash their hands.

The carver would then serve the first mess. This would comprise a range of dishes: meats boiled and roasted, vegetables — including the ubiquitous pottage — along with several sweets. The ewer would serve the drinks from the cupboard. Guests might try small portions of the various dishes and then the first mess was taken away, with the leftovers eaten later by other members of the household. Next, there would often follow a second mess, which included more exquisite items such as game, poultry and fish. After each mess, crumbs and debris would be swept into wicker voiders to leave the tables clean for the next course. A meal would end with a dessert of fruit, cheese or custards and sweet wine. The servants would carefully clear the table and, on special occasions, a fresh clean white tablecloth and towels would

be laid out, with water for the family and guests to wash their hands.

Following the meal, the furniture might be pushed back against the walls to provide space for entertainment, such as gaming, music, dancing, or a bard reciting. Eventually, Robert and Dorothy Wynn would withdraw to their two private rooms, which are situated behind the great chamber in the north range. Both these private rooms had beds, but they also acted as sitting rooms. Similar, but less highly decorated accommodation was provided for guests in another two rooms at the opposite end of the great chamber. There was one more family room, the parlour, situated on the ground floor in the north-east corner of the house. This was probably laid out as another bed-sitting room and may have acted as a more intimate room for receiving guests.

The house offered other facilities for the amusement of the Wynn family and their guests. They might, for example, climb the tower and have a range of prospects over the borough of Conwy, its castle, the river and its ships, with the mountains beyond. The lower courtyard terrace connected with the rear of the gatehouse and led to the top-floor gallery. On wet and cold days, this would have provided a room for gentle exercise, or where the ladies might sew or read. In the summer, the family would walk in the formal gardens laid out around the north side of the house, or perhaps take a stroll on the town walls.

The 1580s were a time of display and conspicuous consumption by the Elizabethan middle and upper classes. The increasing wealth of the period was invested in new houses, rich fittings, household goods, and generous hospitality. The household had to evolve from the much more communal arrangements of the Middle Ages to cope with the increasing desire for privacy and the more sophisticated pastimes of Elizabeth I's reign. Plas Mawr provides a vivid reminder of this period.

*Above: This detail from
Sir Henry Unton's memorial
picture, which shows him
on his death-bed, illustrates
the furnishings of a wealthy
man's bedchamber (National
Portrait Gallery).*

*Opposite: The great chamber
was the ceremonial pivot
of a late sixteenth-century
household. At Plas Mawr the
room has been redecorated
using the original colours
and refurnished according
to the inventory of 1665.*

Plas Mawr and the Elizabethan House

The design and decoration of Plas Mawr was created by a blend of two principal architectural traditions. The first of these influences came from other local buildings of the north Wales gentry. Many aspects of Plas Mawr can be found, for example, about forty years earlier at Robert Wynn's father's house, Gwydir Castle. Similar features can also be found in other early Tudor halls such as Berain, near Denbigh, or Cochwillan, near Bethesda. The second tradition to influence Plas Mawr was the Renaissance style of northern Europe with which Robert was very familiar from his Continental travels.

Such details as the pedimented windows, the crow-stepped gables, and the 'look-out tower' had, by 1576, become quite common in important English houses. Crow-stepped gables and towers can be seen, for instance, in an engraving of Edward VI's coronation procession in London during 1548, whereas pedimented windows and classical columns dominated the main elevation of Somerset House in the Strand, built in 1550. Sir Philip Hoby's house at Bisham Abbey certainly had crow-stepped gables and pedimented windows. It appears to have been Sir Richard Clough who introduced crow-stepped gables into north Wales

Opposite: The gatehouse to Plas Mawr, completed in 1585. The successful use of symmetry, pedimented windows and faceted finials makes the gatehouse a more typical Renaissance building than the main house itself.

Below: Edward VI's coronation procession on Cheapside, London, in 1548. Some houses show the crow-stepped gables and look-out towers fashionable at the time (Society of Antiquaries, London).

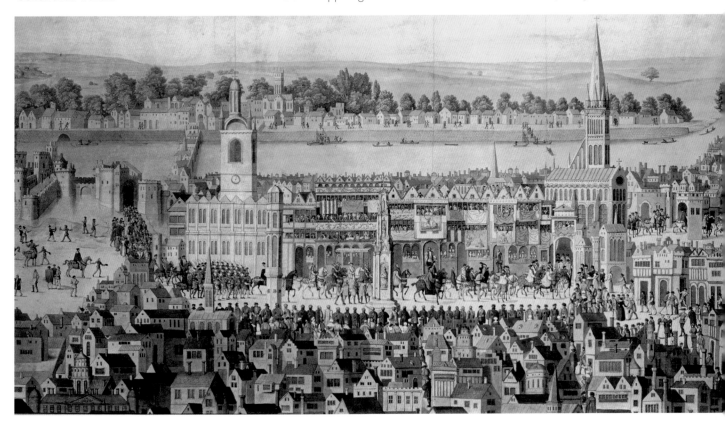

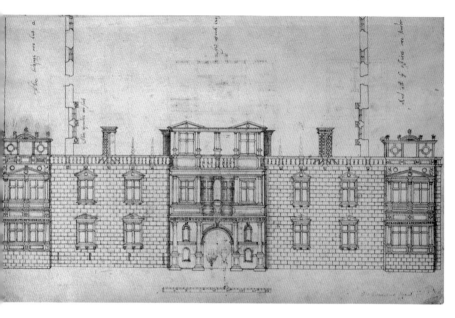

Above: The front elevation of Somerset House in the Strand, built in 1550 (Sir John Soane's Museum).

This house is situated in Stein-am-Rhein on the Swiss/German border. Built in 1567, it has the distinctive crow-stepped gable reminiscent of Plas Mawr. It is a house which can also be compared in size and status to Robert Wynn's home.

in the late 1560s at his houses of Bachegraig and Plas Clough, near Denbigh. The style originated in Flanders, and in many ways Plas Mawr would not look out of place in many of the historic town centres of Belgium, Holland or Germany today.

The plan of the main house at Plas Mawr is basically an adaptation of a traditional rural Elizabethan manor. This ideal layout had to be contained within the limited space offered by the already built-up medieval borough. At first, visitors arriving at the original entrance, which led through the porch and passageway from Crown Lane into the upper courtyard, might have expected to see the hall directly ahead; instead it was tucked to one side. Then, five years after the completion of the main house, Robert Wynn added his splendid gatehouse. In country houses, such gatehouses were commonplace and provided the first stage of the ceremonial approach to a grand house. Plas Mawr is a rare example of adopting such an approach in an urban setting. When complete, visitors would have passed through the gatehouse and then on to a new doorway created in the side of the hall.

Writing in 1577, William Harrison considered that 'three things ... be marvelously altered in England'. They were firstly 'the multitude of chimneys lately erected', which demonstrated the greatly increased number of living rooms within houses. The second was 'the great amendment of lodging', where every level of society sought much greater comfort, particularly with regard to beds and bedding. And thirdly, 'the exchange of vessels', where people were seeking to upgrade wooden vessels and implements to pewter, pewter to silver, and silver to silver gilt. All these trends are demonstrated in the plan and the recorded contents of Plas Mawr.

The hall, the great communal chamber of the Middle Ages, had been relegated to an entrance and servants' dining room. The family apartments were now at first-floor level, focused on the great chamber, with private bed-sitting rooms for Robert and Dorothy Wynn and their guests, all heated by their own fireplaces. These smaller rooms, with their lower ceilings, gave more surfaces for lavish decoration, together with space for rich contents. The rooms on the ground floor, and the cellars, were carefully planned for the more efficient storage and production of food than their medieval predecessors, reflecting the smaller size of Tudor households.

The decoration of the interior represents a concerted effort to establish Robert Wynn's lineage and newly found status. The plaster detailing is full of coats of arms and other emblems. These may have been complemented with painted glass, embroidered clothes, and specially made items of furniture or silver plate. Unlike the exterior, the Renaissance details of the interior, the caryatids, the plaster columns, and the guilloche carvings on the screens, seem rather token additions. Plas Mawr is a celebration of Robert Wynn, his life, his times and his wealth. The result, however, it must be said, is not as sophisticated as contemporary houses which were built by better connected, wealthier and more educated patrons. Longleat

in Wiltshire, for example, which was finally completed by Sir John Thynne (d. 1580) in 1568–72, shows a better understanding of the classical orders of architecture and the use of symmetry. Or if we consider the additions made to Moreton Corbet Castle, Shropshire, in 1579, we see that they are much more boldly ornamented.

Plas Mawr belongs to another quite distinct group of sixteenth-century houses built by the newly emerging Elizabethan middle class. The traditional division between the lords on their country estates and the merchants in the towns had begun to break down by this time. The Tudor middle classes were often professional men, such as lawyers, bankers, surgeons and court officials. Meanwhile, the gentry took a greater interest in trade and industry,

The High Great Chamber at Hardwick Hall, Derbyshire, the most lavishly decorated room surviving from the end of Elizabeth's reign (©NTPL/ Andreas von Einsiedel).

speculating — often with great success — in new entrepreneurial ventures. Wealth was put into new houses, often in fresh locations, such as the edges of towns, on former monastic sites, and on country estates bought by local men who had made good their position.

Many examples appeared around London, where the new houses were built for the first generation of commuters who had offices at court or business in the city. Eastbury Manor in Barking, Essex, built for Clement Sysley and completed in 1572, is one example whose design is often compared to Plas Mawr. The larger towns of the Welsh Marches provide other parallels. Church's Mansion, for instance, was built on the outskirts of Nantwich for Richard Church in 1577, and Whitehall was built within the former precinct of Shrewsbury Abbey in 1578–82 for the lawyer, Robert Prince.

In turn, Plas Mawr was to have a considerable influence on local building in north Wales. Robert Wynn's nephew, Sir John Wynn, took the plaster decoration and stone-carved details to add them to Gwydir Castle. Until it was demolished, the similarities with the Griffith family's town house of Plas Mawr in Caernarfon (built in 1591) were clear. And the new wing added to Hen Blas, the largest town house in Beaumaris, follows the same style.

With the renewed interest in Tudor and Jacobean architecture in the first half of the nineteenth century, the distinctive elements of Plas Mawr's design were adopted by local builders. The designs of the former railway station, the police station, Llys Llewellyn, and the Castlebank Hotel all derive from this source, as does that of the town cinema built as late as 1935. Much further afield, copies of the decorated ceilings were used in Victoria House in the British pavilion at the World's Columbian Exposition in Chicago in 1893.

Plas Mawr can be said to have survived by a series of accidents of history. Its original design and construction stemmed from Robert Wynn's rich and varied early life. His large family, with his children born so late in life, led to a

Above: The now ruinous Elizabethan range at Moreton Corbet Castle, Shropshire. Built in 1579, it was a much more boldly ornamented structure than Plas Mawr (English Heritage).

Right: The timber-framed Church's Mansion at Nantwich in Cheshire was built in 1577. Like Plas Mawr, it is a house typical of those built by the emerging Elizabethan middle class.

Right: Whitehall, Shrewsbury, was built by a successful lawyer in 1578–82. This watercolour by A. E. Everitt (1824–82) shows it in the nineteenth century (Shrewsbury Museums Service).

dissipation of his inheritance as his estate became tied up in legal wrangles. Although the Wynn family lived at Plas Mawr for over eighty years after Robert's death, they had little money to alter or bring the house up to date. Thereafter, for generations, it was let out for a multiplicity of uses. Remarkably, this phase left very little permanent impact on the original fabric. Whilst rooms were subdivided, stairs inserted and new layers of paint added, no major part of the building was lost.

Subsequently, the Royal Cambrian Academy of Art took over the lease for almost a hundred years, preserving and making this wonderful building accessible to the public. Finally, the first systematic conservation programme of Plas Mawr was completed between 1993 and 1997 by Cadw, the historic environment service of the Welsh Assembly Government. The safety of the building has been assured for future generations to appreciate and enjoy its enthralling qualities.

The now demolished Plas Mawr in Caernarfon was originally built for the Griffith family in 1591. This painting by John Buckler (1770–1854) shows the house in 1810. With its crow-stepped gables, its design was a clear reflection of the work of Robert Wynn at Plas Mawr in Conwy (National Library of Wales).

The Decorated Plasterwork

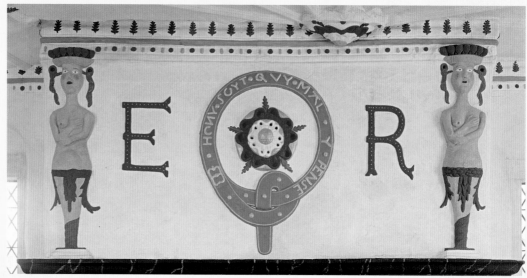

Right: The overmantel in the great chamber, displaying the garter arms.

Below: The eagle, a badge of the Welsh prince, Owain Gwynedd, was adopted as the Wynn family emblem. A severed Englishman's head was the grisly emblem of the Griffith family. The boar represents Katheryn de Berain.

Opposite: The chamber over the brewhouse, with the most elaborate plaster decoration in the house, was probably Robert Wynn's own room.

The decorated plasterwork is one of the glories of Plas Mawr. In all, there are five rooms with decorated ceilings, friezes and overmantels, and two rooms where cornices survive but the ceilings are lost. The most elaborate decoration survives in the parlour and in the two upper chambers in the north range, dated 1577. Here, twenty-two different heraldic emblems are placed within geometrically patterned ceilings and wall-panels. Elizabethans were fascinated with emblems and Sir Geoffrey Whitney wrote in 1586 that an emblem should be 'something obscure to be perceived, whereby when with further consideration it is understood, it may the greater delight the beholder'.

Many of the emblems and badges are of the princes of Gwynedd from whom Robert and his wife Dorothy claimed descent: for example, the standing eagle, the fleur-de-lis, the severed Englishman's head and the stag's head. Others refer to people prominent in north Wales: the Tudor rose, the bear and ragged staff for the earl of Leicester, and the boar for Katheryn de Berain. Others represent local families, such as the owl for the Hookes of Conwy.

The emblems are placed in geometric patterns of ribs or inside engaged classical columns or pilasters; many are derived from pattern books. Every room is embellished with the date and the initials of Robert Wynn and/or of his wife, Dorothy Griffith: sometimes mixed up or shown as mirror images. Fewer emblems were used in the later central and south ranges and greater attention is given to those of the Wynns. A new device also appeared — the caryatid, the partly naked female figure. Originally a Greek classical motif, it became debased through images in pattern books and in the cartoon-like treatment by the plasterer.

The plasterwork confirms the social status of the different rooms. In those rooms where Robert would have entertained his equals or betters — the great chamber and the parlour — the garter and royal arms are given prominence over the fireplace, and the Wynn arms relegated to the ceiling or frieze. In the hall, where he would have met his household, or social inferiors; and in the private bedchambers, the Wynn arms are displayed on the overmantels and the royal badges and other emblems restricted to subservient positions.

The Elizabethan Garden at Plas Mawr

God Almighty first planted a garden. And indeed it is the purest of human pleasures. It is the greatest refreshment to the spirits of man; without which, buildings and palaces are but gross handyworks: and a man shall ever see that when ages grow to civility and elegancy, men come to build stately sooner than to garden finely; as if gardening were the greater perfection.

Francis Bacon (d. 1626) in his essay, *Of Gardens*.

Opposite: The magnificent garden at Llanerch, Denbighshire, was created by Mutton Davies. The summerhouse at Plas Mawr is based on those in the painting (The Bridgeman Art Library © Yale Center for British Art, Paul Mellon Collection, USA).

Elizabethan Gardens in Wales

Wales has a wealth of Elizabethan gentry houses built as a result of the new opportunities and confidence offered to Welshmen by the Tudor dynasty. With these houses went gardens. Medieval pleasure gardens had been small and enclosed; however, Renaissance ideas such as terracing, the use of sculpture, and water features were brought back from the great gardens of France and Italy, and elements of these gradually appeared in the grander gardens of Wales. In his description of Bachegraig, Sir Richard Clough's house in Denbighshire, Richard Fenton records that 'the most uniform and handsomest front is towards a garden, or perhaps what was once a bowling green'. A nineteenth-century painting of Maenan Hall shows a small fenced garden with formal beds and standard trees or shrubs. Further south, on a grand scale, the third earl of Worcester, William Somerset (d. 1589), one of the leading courtiers of the day, had begun the magnificent Tudor gardens at Raglan Castle in Monmouthshire.

None of these developments would have been lost on Robert Wynn and anxious as he was to build a house that reflected his wealth and standing so too was it necessary to create a garden that was appropriate for his position. Here, the family could take walks and retire in seclusion from the rest of the household and the bustle of Conwy's streets.

An artist's impression of the elaborate Tudor gardens created at Raglan Castle in Monmouthshire by William Somerset (d. 1589) (Illustration by Ivan Lapper, 2003).

Robert Wynn's Garden

After Robert Wynn had completed the main house of Plas Mawr in 1580, he continued to acquire land in Conwy. One of his motives was to develop a walled ornamental garden around the north range. This garden was illustrated on a 'bird's-eye view' of Conwy painted around 1600. It shows an irregular enclosure behind Plas Mawr divided into four beds, each laid out in geometrical patterns with one large tree. It is the largest and most complex garden in the town. Other areas are shown with regular patterns of trees, which probably represent orchards. Although this view is probably schematic, it provides helpful clues about how the garden was laid out at this time.

More evidence was revealed by the archaeological excavations that took place before the garden was recreated. These revealed the position of the dairy, through which the garden was entered from the upper courtyard. The dairy had a central passage with a room to either side where the butter and cheese were made. The 1665 inventory also records that the washing was done here. The garden was divided into a small lower terrace and a large upper terrace. The original stone-lined drains in these terraces survive beneath the gravel surface and parts of the original enclosing stone walls also survive on the south, west and north sides of the garden.

The remaining section of the original area of the garden is now hidden below the Royal Cambrian Academy of Art's gallery.

The Recreated Garden

Alongside the archaeological evidence and the drawing of 1600, a wide range of relict gardens, garden structures and ornaments associated with other Elizabethan houses survive in north Wales. These too have provided sources of inspiration for the recreation of the garden.

As in the furnished rooms of Plas Mawr, Cadw has chosen to recreate the garden using what is believed to be the original Elizabethan structure of the garden but decorated and planted at the time of the inventory taken in 1665. This provides a greater range of plants than would have been available eighty years earlier, and allows contemporary documents from elsewhere in Wales to be used to help furnish and plant the garden. For instance, the Wynn papers tell that 'slivers of tamarisk' were taken from Piers Griffith's garden in Conwy to Gwydir in 1625. More particularly, we can draw on *The Garden Book of Sir Thomas Hanmer*. Sir Thomas Hanmer (d. 1678) of Bettisfield, near Wrexham, was Wales's greatest horticulturalist and one of the finest of the day, exchanging letters and plants with such distinguished nurserymen as the king's gardener, John Rose (d. 1677), John Evelyn (d. 1706) and John Rea (d. 1681). The book is full of practical advice on the cultivation of the full range of plants available at the time including exotics being imported from the Mediterranean and the Americas. Hanmer had a particular love of tulips and cultivated a very wide range of fruit trees trained on the walls of his garden. One of the sections of his book is headed: 'Here are also added Remembrances of what is to bee done in a GARDEN every Moneth of the Yeare, and what plants are usually in FLOWER in each Moneth in England', practical advice that remains true today.

Above: A detail from a 'bird's-eye view' of Conwy in about 1600, showing gardens laid out behind Plas Mawr. Part of this area is now occupied by the gallery of the Royal Cambrian Academy of Art (By permission of the marquess of Salisbury, Hatfield House, CPM 1/62).

Opposite: The upper courtyard. The garden is reached by crossing this courtyard and walking through the dairy façade.

The Garden Book of Sir Thomas Hanmer *is a rich source of information about the plants in favour in the seventeenth century. This portrait of Sir Thomas (d. 1678) is by the eminent artist, Sir Anthony van Dyck (1599–1641)(Trustees of the Weston Park Foundation, UK/Bridgeman Art Library).*

The lower terrace lies behind the façade of the dairy. From here, steps lead to the upper terrace with its summerhouse and geometric flowerbeds.

The Lower Terrace

The lower terrace was entered from the upper courtyard via the central passage in the dairy. The position of this passage is now marked with pitched slate slabs in the gravel. The windows either side of the doorway would have lit the rooms where the butter and cheese were made.

Morello cherry trees are planted on the shaded side of the south wall and a peach and a nectarine against the warm upper terrace revetment walls. A lead planter based on seventeenth-century examples, but incorporating emblems in the decorated plasterwork in the house, is planted with red lobelia and lychnis, blue campanula and anchusa and a yucca. The flowerpots are based on late seventeenth-century examples excavated in the gardens of Tredegar House, Newport, and they are planted with the range of herbs used in the kitchen, as well as pinks (dianthus).

The Upper Terrace

The revetment wall and steps to the upper terrace are based on the surviving structures in the lower courtyard. The form of the little summerhouse is derived from the pavilions in a painting of the gardens at Llanerch, Denbighshire (p. 38), and the Wynn eagle pierced through its door emphasizes Robert Wynn's fascination with emblems and badges. The layout of the garden beds on the upper terrace is based on the ceiling designs in the house and on contemporary illustrations.

The upper terrace garden is contained on each side within lines of wooden trellis capped by artificial-looking details — in the Dutch Mannerist style — woven with hazel rods. These are planted with honeysuckle, clematis and jasmine. Against the rear wall are contemporary varieties of roses. The geometric beds are planted with colourful seventeenth-century varieties, such as red lobelia, lychnis and lilies; purple campanula, geranium, aquilegia and iris; blue lupins, anemones and anchusa; white daisies and cardamine; yellow iris, trollius and lupins; pink dianthus, tamarisk and saxifrage; as well as seventeenth-century tulip varieties and evergreens, such as yucca and phillyrea.

Above: Fruit trees have been trained on the walls of the lower terrace.

Far left: A lead planter commissioned for the garden incorporates emblems found in the plasterwork in the house.

Left: The upper terrace flower beds have been planted with varieties popular in the seventeenth century.

Further Reading

Malcolm Airs, *The Tudor and Jacobean Country House: A Building History* (Stroud 1995).

Arthur Baker and Herbert Baker, *Plas Mawr, Conway, N. Wales* (London 1888).

A. D. Carr, 'The Affairs of Robert Wynn', *Transactions of the Caernarvonshire Historical Society*, **49** (1988), 151–72.

Nicholas Cooper, *Houses of the Gentry 1480–1680* (New Haven and London 1999).

Mark Girouard, *Life in the English Country House* (New Haven and London 1978).

William Harrison, *The Description of England* (1587), reprinted edition, edited by G. Edelen (Washington 1994).

Felicity Heal and Clive Holmes, *The Gentry in England and Wales, 1500–1700* (London 1994).

Maurice Howard, *The Early Tudor Country House: Architecture and Politics 1490–1550* (London 1987).

J. Gwynfor Jones, editor, *The History of the Wynn Family and Memoirs [by] Sir John Wynn* (Llandysul 1990).

J. Gwynfor Jones, *The Wynn Family of Gwydir* (Aberystwyth 1995).

Royal Commission on the Ancient and Historical Monuments in Wales, *An Inventory of the Ancient Monuments in Caernarvonshire, Volume I: East* (London 1956), 58–64.

Peter Smith, *Houses of the Welsh Countryside*, 2nd edition (London 1988).

R. C. Turner, 'Robert Wynn and the Building of Plas Mawr, Conwy', *National Library of Wales Journal*, **29.2** (1995), 177–209.

Glanmor Williams, *Recovery, Reorientation and Reformation: Wales c. 1415–1642* (Oxford 1987); reprinted in paperback as, *Renewal and Reformation: Wales c. 1415–1642* (Oxford 1993).

Plas Mawr

Garden Plan

Some of the flowers to be seen in the parterre beds:

Aquilegia vulgaris

Trollius europaeus

Cardamine pratensis

Geranium sanguineum

Lychnis chalcedonica

Saxifraga umbrosa

Anchusa azurea

Campanula persicifolia

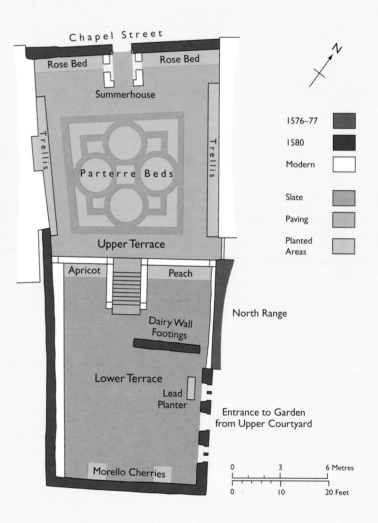

Chapel Street

Rose Bed   Rose Bed

Summerhouse

Trellis   Trellis

Parterre Beds

Upper Terrace

Apricot   Peach

North Range

Dairy Wall Footings

Lower Terrace

Lead Planter

Entrance to Garden from Upper Courtyard

Morello Cherries

N

1576–77
1580
Modern

Slate
Paving
Planted Areas

0   3   6 Metres
0   10   20 Feet